SEASONS OF THE YEAR

Fall

by Rebecca Pettiford

BELLWETHER MEDIA • MINNEAPOLIS, MN

Note to Librarians, Teachers, and Parents:

Blastoff! Readers are carefully developed by literacy experts and combine standards-based content with developmentally appropriate text.

Level 1 provides the most support through repetition of high-frequency words, light text, predictable sentence patterns, and strong visual support.

Level 2 offers early readers a bit more challenge through varied simple sentences, increased text load, and less repetition of high-frequency words.

Level 3 advances early-fluent readers toward fluency through increased text and concept load, less reliance on visuals, longer sentences, and more literary language.

Level 4 builds reading stamina by providing more text per page, increased use of punctuation, greater variation in sentence patterns, and increasingly challenging vocabulary.

Level 5 encourages children to move from "learning to read" to "reading to learn" by providing even more text, varied writing styles, and less familiar topics.

Whichever book is right for your reader, Blastoff! Readers are the perfect books to build confidence and encourage a love of reading that will last a lifetime!

This edition first published in 2018 by Bellwether Media, Inc.

No part of this publication may be reproduced in whole or in part without written permission of the publisher. For information regarding permission, write to Bellwether Media, Inc., Attention: Permissions Department, 5357 Penn Avenue South, Minneapolis, MN 55419.

Library of Congress Cataloging-in-Publication Data

Names: Pettiford, Rebecca, author.
Title: Fall / by Rebecca Pettiford.
Description: Minneapolis, MN : Bellwether Media, 2018 | Series: Blastoff!
  Readers: Seasons of the Year | Includes bibliographical references and
  index. | Audience: K-3.
Identifiers: LCCN 2017029523 | ISBN 9781626177604 (hardcover : alk. paper)
  | ISBN 9781681034652 (ebook) | ISBN 9781618913012 (pbk. : alk. paper)
Subjects: LCSH: Autumn–Juvenile literature.
Classification: LCC QB637.7 .P43 2018 | DDC 508.2–dc23
LC record available at https://lccn.loc.gov/2017029523

Editor: Christina Leaf   Designer: Josh Brink

Printed in the United States of America, North Mankato, MN.

Table of Contents

Falling Leaves

Brrr! The air is cool and crisp. It smells like earth.

Colorful leaves tumble to the
ground. They crunch under
feet. This is fall!

When Is Fall?

The season of fall starts after summer. It ends as winter begins.

It is also called autumn.

In the **Northern Hemisphere**, fall starts in September.

Earth's Position in Fall

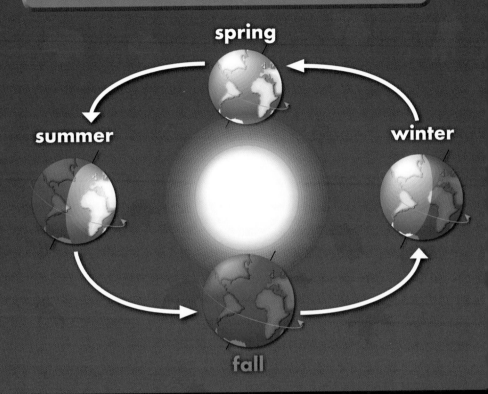

spring

summer

winter

fall

Earth's tilt allows the Northern and Southern Hemispheres to get equal daylight in fall. Days get shorter as winter gets closer.

The main fall months are September, October, and November.

Fall Weather

In fall, the days get shorter as Earth **tilts** away from the sun.

When there is less sunlight, the air gets colder. **Frost** forms overnight.

frost

Fall weather changes quickly.
Clouds often cover the sky,
and the wind picks up.

Hurricane Watch

Peak Hurricane Season:
August 20 to October 20

Where Hurricanes Form in October

| highest risk | high risk | low risk | hurricane movement |

Many **hurricanes** happen in September and October. Late fall often brings the first snow.

Plants and Animals in Fall

Fall is known for colorful leaves. **Deciduous** trees use sunlight to make green leaves.

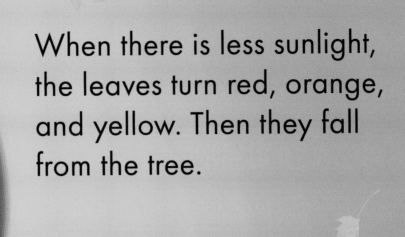

When there is less sunlight, the leaves turn red, orange, and yellow. Then they fall from the tree.

deciduous tree

15

Animals use fall to prepare for winter. They **hoard** food while it is plentiful.

cardinal

To keep warm, some animals eat
a lot to build up fat. Others grow
thicker fur.

Geese honk while flying overhead. They are **migrating** south where it is warm.

migrating geese

marmot

Some animals get **burrows** ready for **hibernation**. They will sleep through the winter.

apple **harvest**

People **harvest** crops like
pumpkins and apples in fall.
Children start school.

Families carve **jack-o'-lanterns** and rake leaves. They enjoy fall fun!

Glossary

burrows—holes or tunnels that some animals dig for homes

deciduous—having leaves that fall off every year

frost—a thin layer of ice that forms on the ground or on plants when the air becomes cold

harvest—to gather or pick crops

hibernation—a state of sleeping or resting, usually in winter

hoard—to gather and hide a large amount of something

hurricanes—large, powerful storms with swirling winds that form over warm ocean waters

jack-o'-lanterns—pumpkins for Halloween that have faces cut into them and are lit from inside

migrating—traveling from one place to another, often with the seasons

Northern Hemisphere—the half of the globe that lies north of the equator; the equator is an imaginary line around Earth.

tilts—slants or tips

To Learn More

AT THE LIBRARY
Herrington, Lisa M. *How Do You Know It's Fall?*
New York, N.Y.: Children's Press, 2014.

Moon, Walt K. *Fall is Fun!* Minneapolis, Minn.:
Lerner Publications, 2017.

Pak, Kenard. *Goodbye Summer, Hello Autumn.*
New York, N.Y.: Henry Holt and Company, 2016.

ON THE WEB
Learning more about
fall is as easy as 1, 2, 3.

1. Go to www.factsurfer.com.

2. Enter "fall"into the
   search box.

3. Click the "Surf" button and you will see a
   list of related web sites.

With factsurfer.com, finding more
information is just a click away.

Index

The images in this book are reproduced through the courtesy of: Anteromite, front cover; Olesia Bilkei, p. 4; skynesher, p. 5; Michael Wick, p. 6; seawhisper, p. 7; Miao Liao, p. 8; Designua, p. 9; Rabbitt, p. 10; photolinc, p. 11; dugdax, p. 12; David Boutin, p. 14; Kuznetsova Ganna, p. 15; Patrik Mezirka, p. 16; germip, p. 16 (right); Marc Kirby, p. 17; photosbyjimn, p. 18; northallertonman, p. 19; Barrett & MacKay/ Alamy, p. 20, Sergey Novikov, p. 21.

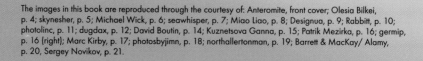